Passport to Transport Songbook

Frances Turnbull

Copyright © 2018 Frances Turnbull

Passport to Transport Song Book
All rights reserved
Musicaliti Publishing, Bolton, UK

ISBN: 978-1907935817

www.musicaliti.co.uk

Contents

Ukulele Tuning and Chords	4
Trains	8
Boats	12
Ships	16
Cars	20
Buses	24
Bicycles	28
Planes	32
Rockets	36
Pictures and music notes 1	41
Pictures and music notes 2	43
Write your own song	45

Passport to Transport Song Book

Ukulele Chords

Ukuleles are small, accessible and relatively cheap instruments that can be used to play the accompaniment to many songs.

Each string should be tuned to specific notes (can be found on tuned instruments like xylophones, pianos or recorders etc.). The standard ukulele tuning is:

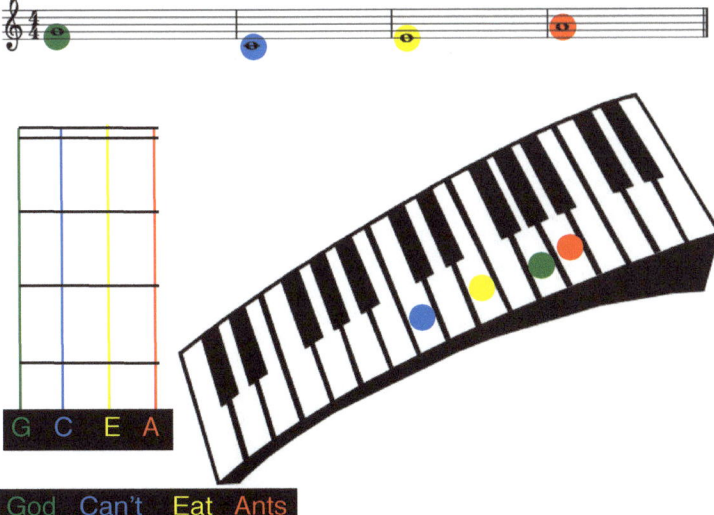

God Can't Eat Ants

By placing your fingers on the frets at the positions on the pictures, (between the lines), you change the sound of the strings into chords when strummed altogether.

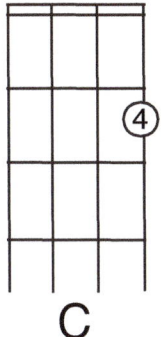
C

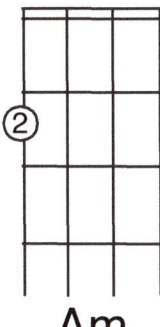
Am

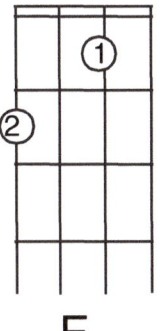
F

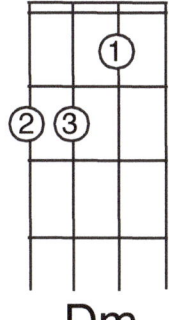
Dm

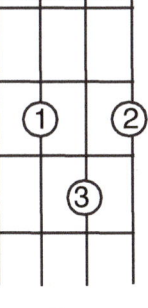
G

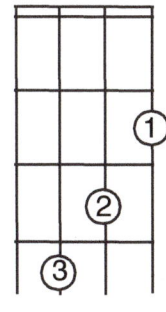
Em

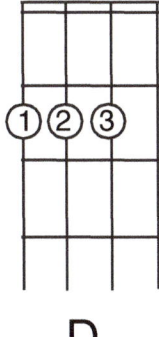
D

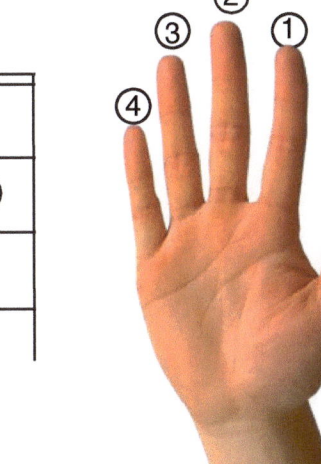

Fast or slow? How shall we go?

Frances Turnbull

LET'S GO BY TRAIN

600BC - The rutway was the first version of a train that the ancient Greeks and Romans used to move ships across land; a pathway made of parallel stone blocks!

DID YOU KNOW:
Train horns are based on MUSICAL CHORDS?
Passenger trains are based on the major 6th interval because it is associated with warm, welcoming feelings (e.g the first two notes of "My Bonnie lies over the Ocean").

Can you find the music notes hidden in this picture in the music on the next page?

Frances Turnbull

1804 - The first steam locomotive railway known as Penydarren or "Pen-y-Darren" locomotive was built by Richard Trevithick, hauled iron from Merthyr Tydfil to Abercynon, Wales. It carried 10 tons of iron!

DID YOU KNOW:
The sound of freight train horns are based on the diminished 7th interval, the music notes often used in scary films, because it sounds so unsettling? This helps people keep away from these fast and potentially dangerous trains!

Can you find the music notes hidden in this picture in the music on the next page?

Passport to Transport Song Book

No one in the kitchen
Passport to Transport

No one in the kit-chen but Di - nah, Di - nah,

no one in the kit-chen but me I know,

No one in the kit-chen but Di - nah, Di - nah,

strum-ming on the old ban - jo.

Frances Turnbull

LET'S GO BY BOAT

Canoe or kayak - In a canoe, the paddler must kneel or sit and paddle with one blade on two paddles. In a kayak, the paddler sits with their legs straight out, and the paddle has blades on both ends!

DID YOU KNOW:
"Steamboat Willie" was the first cartoon featuring Mickey Mouse? It was also the first time that anyone had added music and talking after the film was made!

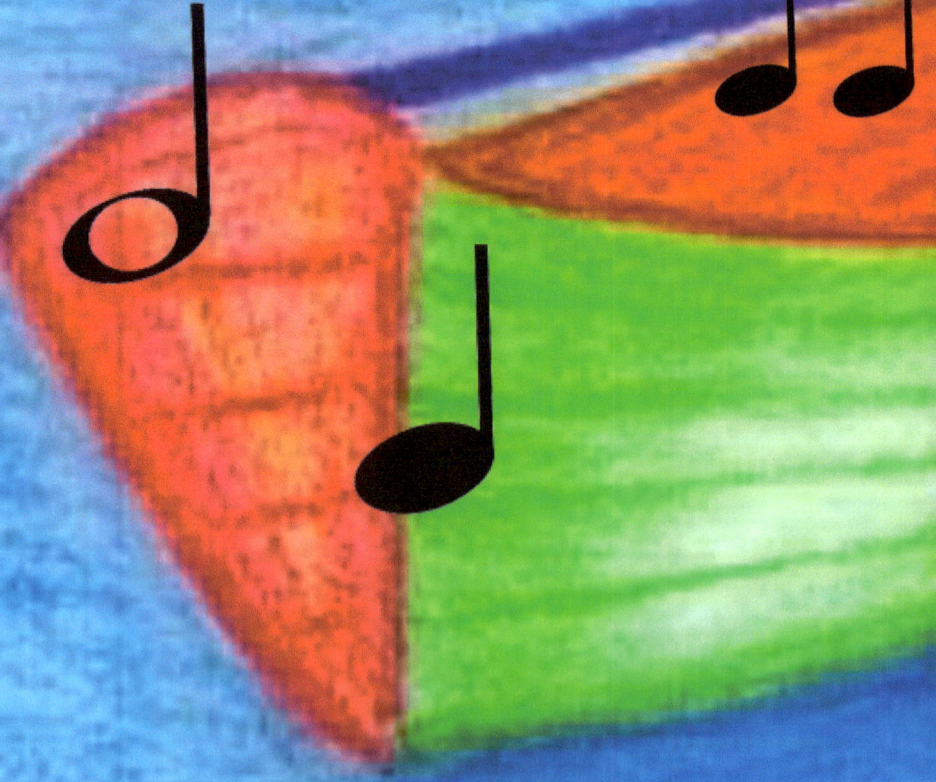

Can you find the music notes hidden in this picture in the music on the next page?

Passport to Transport Song Book

Charlie over the Ocean
Passport to Transport

Char-lie o-ver the o-cean, Char-lie o-ver the o-cean,

Char-lie o-ver the sea, Char-lie o-ver the sea,

Char-lie caught a big fish, Char-lie caught a big fish,

can't catch me, can't catch me!

Frances Turnbull

8200-7600BC - The oldest boat ever found is called the Pesse canoe, in the Netherlands. It was made out of a hollowed out tree trunk!

DID YOU KNOW:
Boats use sound signals to tell others what they are doing? One short blast means "I'm passing you on my left", two short blast means "I'm passing you on my right", and three short blasts means, "I'm reversing"!

Can you find the music notes hidden in this picture in the music on the next page?

Frances Turnbull

LET'S GO BY SHIP

3000BC - The first ships were made by using animal skins as sails, and helped people travel further than ever!

DID YOU KNOW:
The hymn "Amazing Grace" was written by a sailor who worked in the slave trade. After he nearly died a few times, he stopped doing bad things because he said that God had saved him through "Amazing Grace"!

Can you find the music notes hidden in this picture in the music on the next page?

Frances Turnbull

1912 - The Titanic, nicknamed "*the unsinkable ship*", sank on 15 April, and the musicians kept playing music to try to keep the passengers calm, right until it sank!

DID YOU KNOW:
The London Symphony Orchestra was originally booked to play on the Titanic? It had to be replaced at the last minute because of the delays in building the Titanic!

Can you find the music notes hidden in this picture in the music on the next page?

Bobby Shafto
Passport to Transport

Frances Turnbull

LET'S GO BY CAR

1886 - The car as we know it was first invented in Germany by Karl Benz (Mercedes Benz)!

DID YOU KNOW:
Car engines sound different because of EXPLOSIONS in the engines? Sports cars fire faster at higher frequencies than everyday cars, giving their engines a growling quality!

Can you find the music notes hidden in this picture in the music on the next page?

I had a car
Passport to Transport

Lyrics by F Turnbull

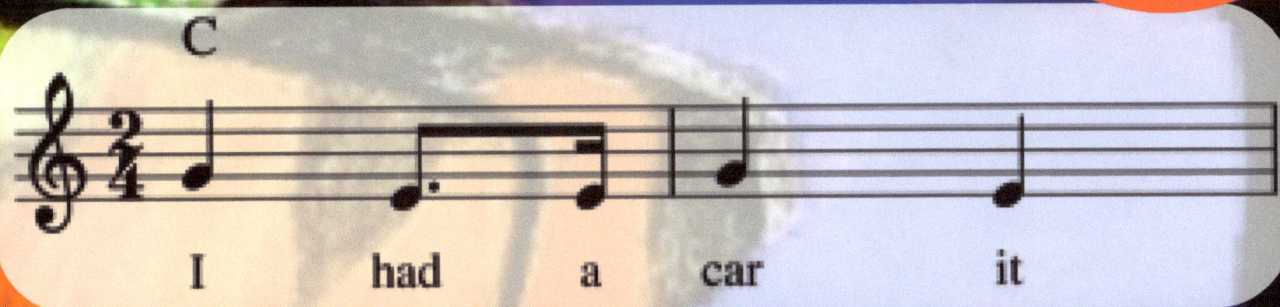

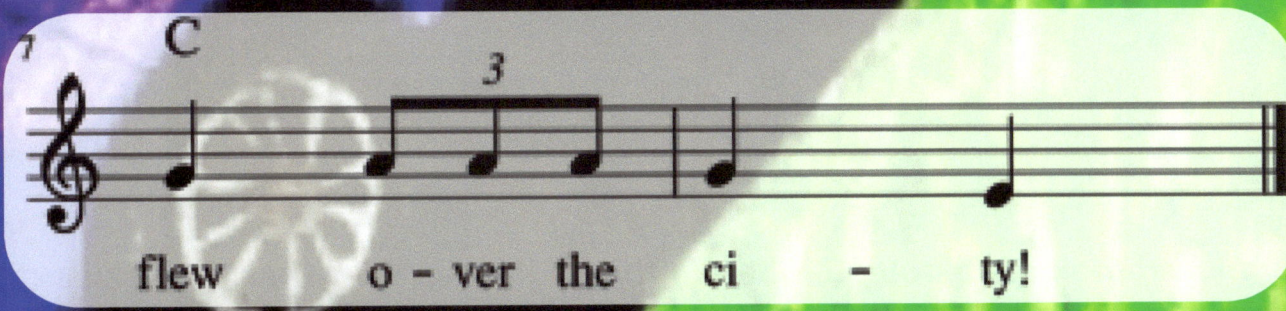

Passport to Transport Song Book

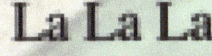
La La La
Passport to Transport

Lyrics by F Turnbull

La la la,

where is my car,

dri - ving on the mo - tor way,

la, la, la!

Frances Turnbull

LET'S GO BY BUS

1800's - The first buses were pulled by horses, and were called horse-buses!

DID YOU KNOW:
Bus horns are usually 2 notes played at the SAME time? This is because they are louder together than one note-by itself!

Can you find the music notes hidden in this picture in the music on the next page?

Buses go fast

Passport to Transport

Lyrics by F Turnbull

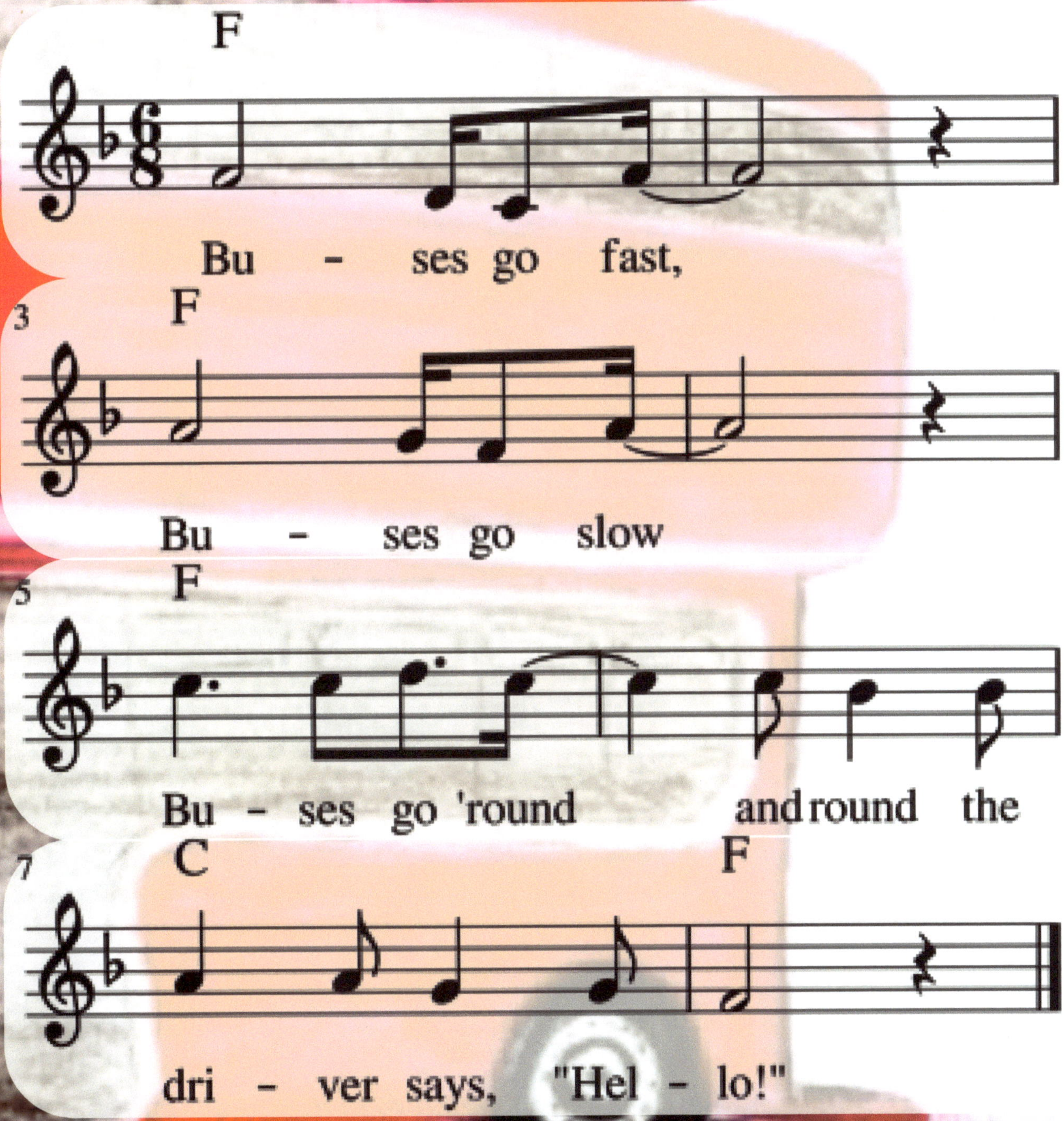
F
Bu - ses go fast,
3 F
Bu - ses go slow
5 F
Bu - ses go 'round and round the
7 C F
dri - ver says, "Hel - lo!"

Frances Turnbull

1955 - One of the most famous buses is the one that Rosa Parks rode. She refused to give her seat up for a white man, helping to make the law equal for all people!

DID YOU KNOW:
Bus horns have been used in MUSICAL works? Each one that they used played a different tune!

Can you find the music notes hidden in this picture in the music on the next page?

Passport to Transport Song Book

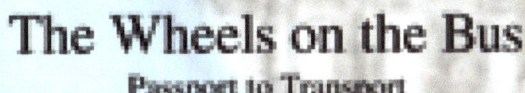
The Wheels on the Bus
Passport to Transport

The wheels on the bus go round and round,

round and round, round and round, the

wheels on the bus go round and round,

all day long!

27

Frances Turnbull

LET'S GO BY BICYCLE

1870s - The Pennyfarthing (names for different size coins in England) was the first to use wire spokes instead of wood!

DID YOU KNOW:
Bicycle BELLS were invented in 1877? It was invented by John Richard Dedicoat from Birmingham, who also invented a pencil-sharpening machine!

Can you find the music notes hidden in this picture in the music on the next page?

Bought me a bike
Passport to Transport

Bought me a bike, the bike pleased me, I

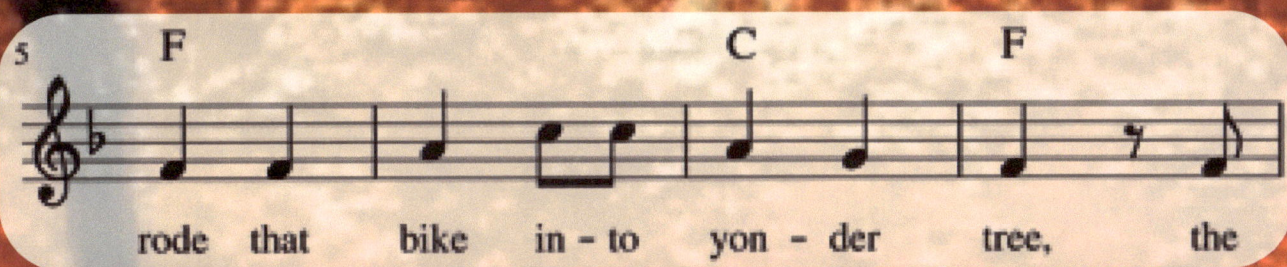
rode that bike in-to yon-der tree, the

bike went sma-shi-ty, sma-shi-ty, sma-shi-ty

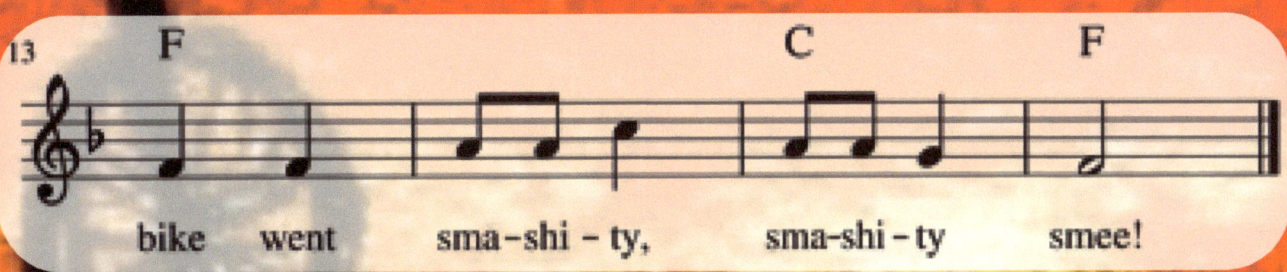
bike went sma-shi-ty, sma-shi-ty smee!

Frances Turnbull

1912 - The very first vehicle with 2 wheels was called the "Dandy horse", invented by Baron Karl von Drais, and it had no pedals, like a balance bike!

DID YOU KNOW:
Bicycle bells were used in POP songs? They can be heard in songs by the Beachboys (*You still believe in me*) and Queen (*Bicycle Race*)!

Can you find the music notes hidden in this picture in the music on the next page?

Passport to Transport Song Book

Cycle Cycle
Passport to Transport

Lyrics by F Turnbull

Cycle, cycle, bi-cycle cy-cle, all jump up!

Cy-cle, cy-cle, bi-cycle cy-cle, all jump down!

Cy-cle, cy-cle, bicycle cy-cle, all jump in!

Cycle, cycle, bicycle cy-cle, all jump out!

Frances Turnbull

LET'S GO BY PLANE

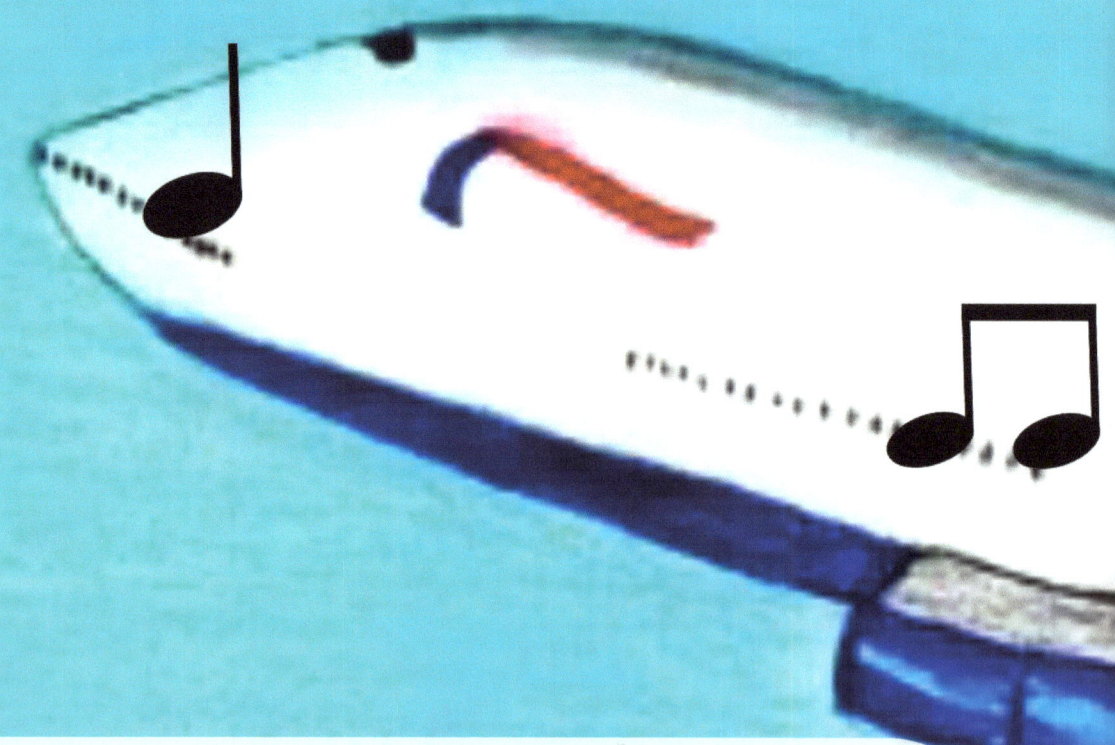

1903 - The first ever airplane was invented by the Wright brothers and flew for 12 seconds!

DID YOU KNOW:
Airplanes make many strange NOISES? The humming when you board the plane is the auxiliary power at the back of the plane that keeps the lights on while the main engines are off!

Can you find the music notes hidden in this picture in the music on the next page?

Passport to Transport Song Book

Hey Aeroplane
Passport to Transport

Lyrics by F Turnbull

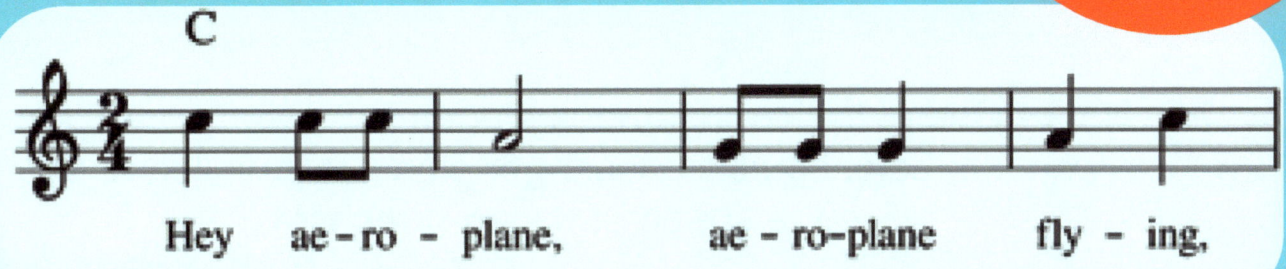

Hey ae-ro-plane, ae-ro-plane fly-ing,

hey ae-ro-plane, fly-ing a-round,

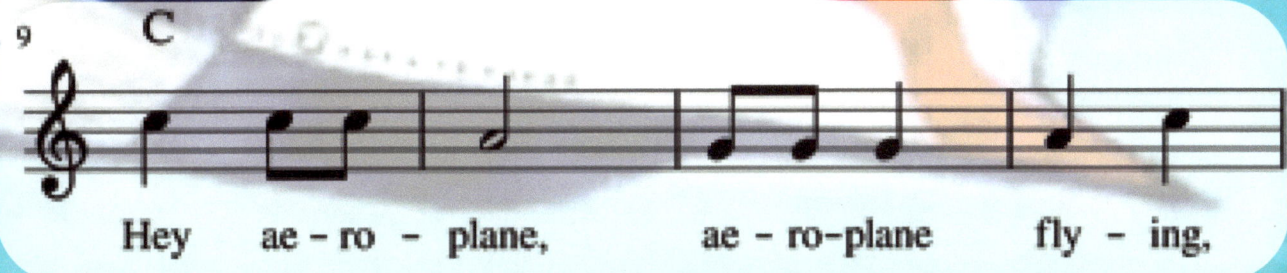

Hey ae-ro-plane, ae-ro-plane fly-ing,

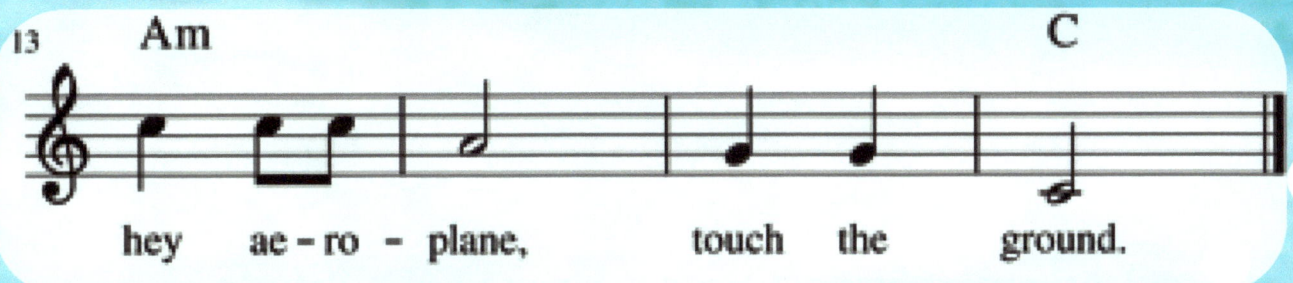

hey ae-ro-plane, touch the ground.

1969 - One of the most famous planes is the Concorde, and it was the fastest public passenger plane! It travelled at over twice the speed of sound (Mach 2.04)!

DID YOU KNOW:
Airplanes sound like they BARK? When they travel on the ground, they only use one engine and the barking sound is a machine that balances the pressure!

Can you find the music notes hidden in this picture in the music on the next page?

In a Plane

Passport to Transport

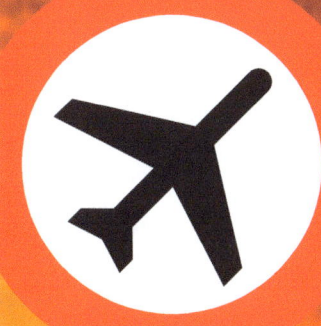

Lyrics by F Turnbull

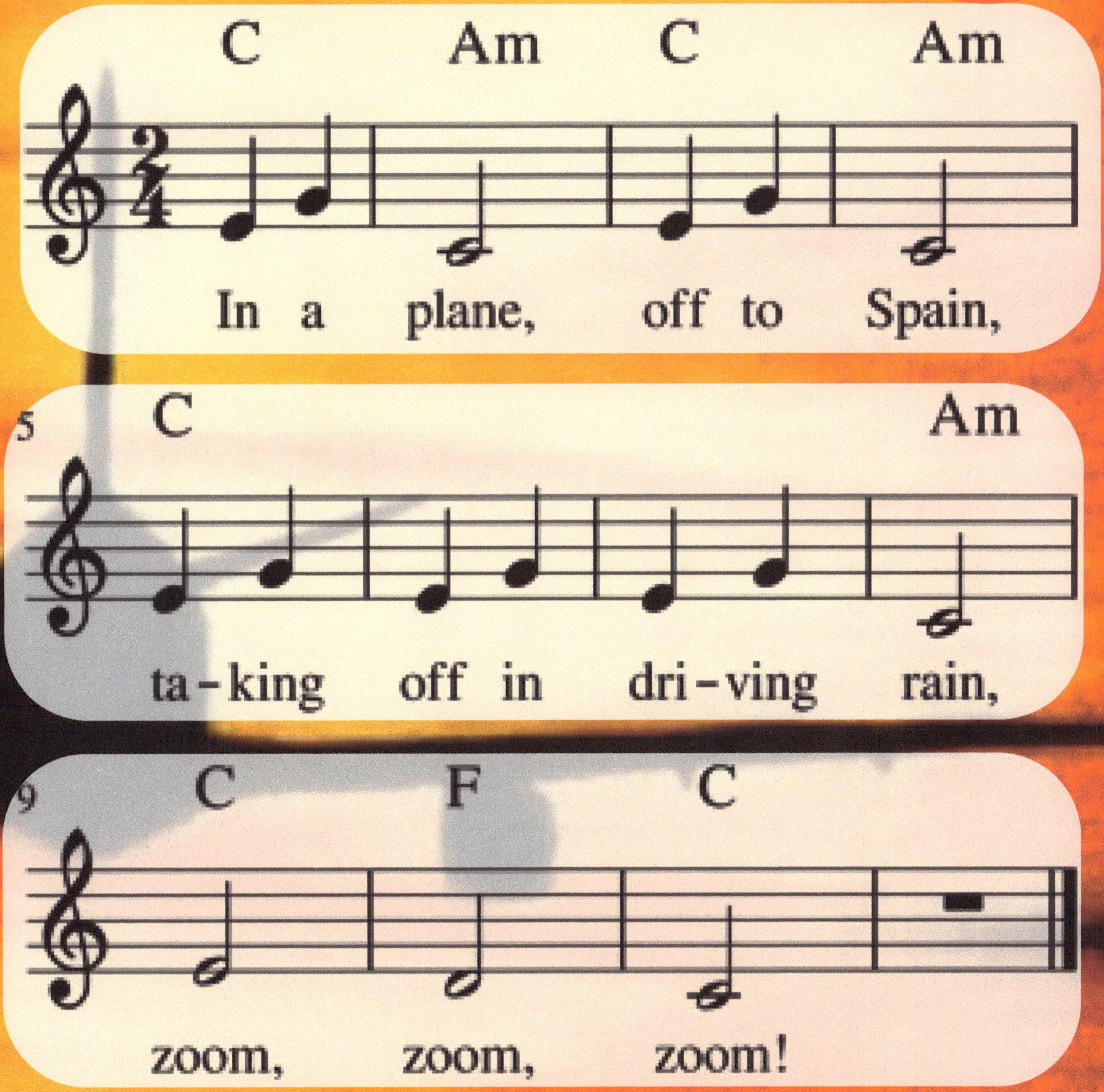
C Am C Am
In a plane, off to Spain,
5 C Am
ta-king off in dri-ving rain,
9 C F C
zoom, zoom, zoom!

Frances Turnbull

LET'S GO BY ROCKET

1961 - The first human in space was Yuri Gagarin, a Soviet pilot and cosmonaut. His Vostok spacecraft orbitted the earth on 12 April!

DID YOU KNOW:
The first communication Yuri sent back to earth was a SONG? He sang *My Homeland Hears* by Shostakovich!

Can you find the music notes hidden in this picture in the music on the next page?

Frances Turnbull

1969 - Apollo 10 was the second rocket to orbit the moon, travelling at a record 24,791 miles per hour!

DID YOU KNOW:
As they got nearer the moon, the astronauts talked about hearing "strange MUSIC"? It was radio interference with the other spacecraft that they took up with them!

Can you find the music notes hidden in this picture in the music on the next page?

Aiken Drum
Passport to Transport

Lyrics by F Turnbull

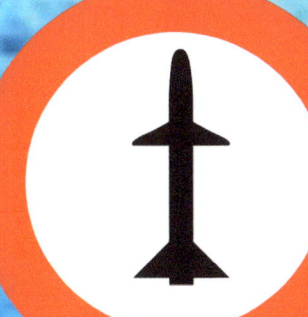

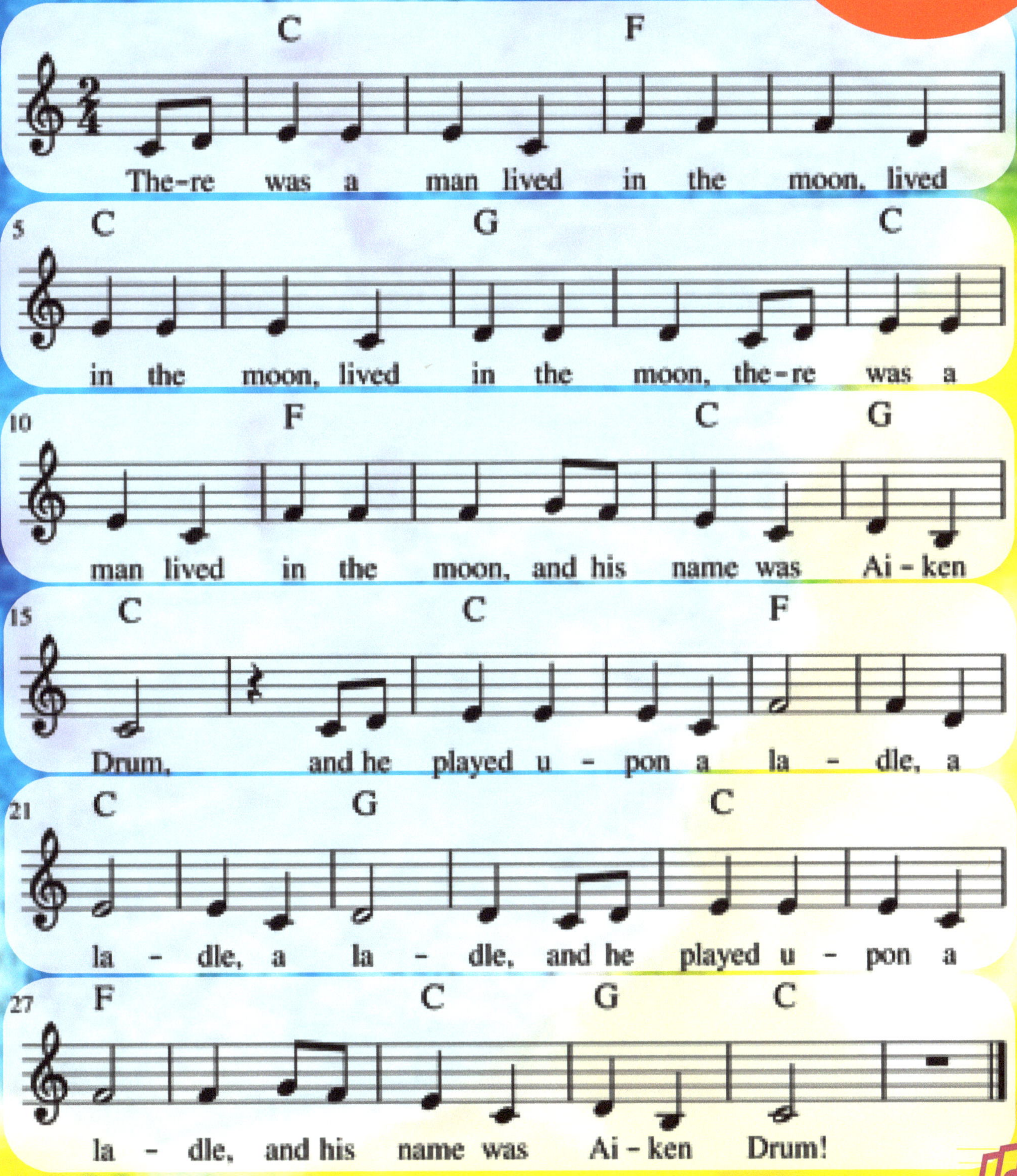

These are the music notes and pictures that we used in our songs!

These are the music notes and pictures that we used in our songs!

My Song

Now use the music or pictures from the previous pages to make up your own song!

The End

Have you seen our other books?

Music Gone Wild Song Book:
Animal Songs for Ukulele
ISBN 9781907935688

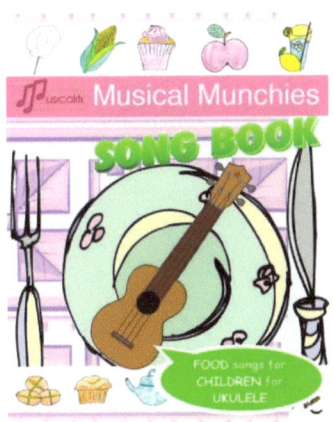

Musical Munchies Song Book:
Food Songs for Ukulele
ISBN 9781907787

Magical Musical Kingdom Song Book:
Magical Songs for Ukulele
ISBN 9781907935770

Goodies for Guitar:
90 songs for beginners
ISBN 9781907935695

Goodies for Guitar: Lvl 1
18 songs for beginners
ISBN 9781907935701

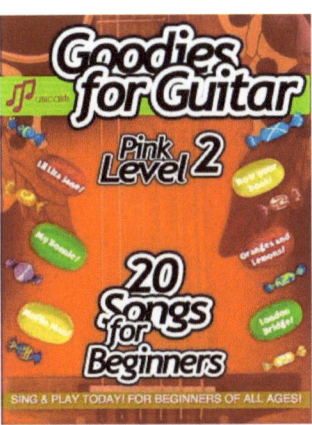

Goodies for Guitar: Lvl 2
20 songs for beginners
ISBN 9781907935718

Sharks, Fish, Shells
Music sessions for 2-4s
ISBN 9781907935633

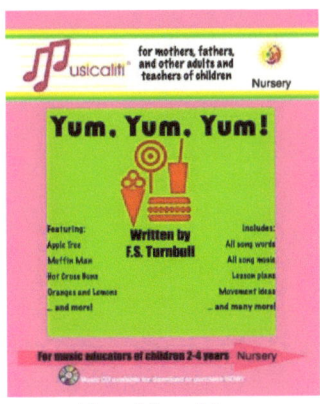

Yum Yum Yum
Music sessions for 2s-4s
ISBN 9781907935206

Magical Musical Kingdom
Music sessions for 2s-4s
ISBN 9781907935152

FIND US ON:

www.ingramcontent.com/pod-product-compliance
Lightning Source LLC
Chambersburg PA
CBHW041534040426
42446CB00002B/90